The SUGGS BOOK of FAMILY TALES

Real-Life Stories of Wit and Wisdom

ROB SUGGS

InterVarsity Press
Downers Grove, Illinois

InterVarsity Press
P.O. Box 1400, Downers Grove, IL 60515-1426
World Wide Web: www.ivpress.com
E-mail: mail@ivpress.com

InterVarsity Press® *is the book-publishing division of InterVarsity Christian Fellowship/USA*®*, a student movement active on campus at hundreds of universities, colleges and schools of nursing in the United States of America, and a member movement of the International Fellowship of Evangelical Students. For information about local and regional activities, write Public Relations Dept., InterVarsity Christian Fellowship/USA, 6400 Schroeder Rd., P.O. Box 7895, Madison, WI 53707-7895, or visit the IVCF website at <www.ivcf.org>.*

All Scripture quotations, unless otherwise indicated, are taken from the Holy Bible, New International Version®. NIV®. *Copyright* ©*1973, 1978, 1984 by International Bible Society. Used by permission of Zondervan Publishing House. All rights reserved.*

Design: Cindy Kiple

Cover Images: Steve Murez/Getty Images

Interior Images: Cindy Kiple

ISBN 0-8308-2369-7

Printed in Canada ∞

Library of Congress Cataloging-in-Publication Data

Suggs, Rob.

  The Suggs book of family tales: real-life stories of wit and wisdom/
Rob Suggs.

    p. cm.
  ISBN 0-8308-2369-7 (hardcover: alk. paper)
  1. Suggs. Rob. 2. Suggs family. 3. Christian biography—United
States. I. Title.
  BR1725.S845A3 2004
  277.3'083'0922—dc22

                                                       2003025925

P	15	14	13	12	11	10	9	8	7	6	5	4	3	2	1
Y	13	12	11	10	09	08	07	06	05	04					

For my brothers

Jim, Steve and Joe

CONTENTS

I

MY BOD IS ODD

I was born right-handed.

That is to say, I began life with right-handed tendencies but was converted at a young age to the left-handed persuasion. On the one hand, I still throw the ball with my right; on the other hand, I write and draw with my left. I eat with the hand (or foot) closest to the food at any given moment. Admittedly this is a confusing state of affairs. I want you to hear my explanation firsthand, or at least as the story has been handed down to me.

I was in fourth grade when I began to grasp that I differed from other children. Specifically I noticed I had a non-participatory right thumb. I couldn't bend it at the joint without using other fingers to manually flex it. The thumb was also considerably smaller and less muscular than its leftward counterpart. My bod was odd, for my thumb was dumb.

I sought an explanation from my father. "Dad," I asked, "what's up with my right thumb?" I demonstrated my digital inflexibility.

Dad lowered his newspaper, wrinkled his brow and scrutinized my thumb for a moment. "It hasn't gotten enough exercise," he ruled. Then he picked up his newspaper and resumed reading. The explanation was good enough for me.

The next day was Show and Tell in Miss Haslett's class. We Suggs boys were always at our best during Show and Tell, which we saw as a vehicle for creative expression. This book, I suppose, is a form of Show and Tell.

On this particular day, Jennie shared a postcard from her uncle in Europe. Tommy brought a robin's nest. Mary Sue had a conch shell from her family's beach vacation. And me, I had my thumb. I shared my healthy, all-American left thumb, then depicted my right as a mutant monstrosity. "It won't do what my mind tells it to," I said. "Maybe aliens are controlling it. Maybe someday the whole hand will come free and start *strangling people!*" Jennie screamed. The boys all sang out, "Cool!"

I walked around and let everyone touch my alien thumb. Mary Sue almost fainted. That was the best part: I was guaranteed girl-free for the rest of fourth grade. Until that school day ended, kids would be shaking their legs, fidgeting to change postures and doing all they could to avoid losing the use of important body sections. Tommy told me, "You shouldn't have let that thumb freeze, man."

Miss Haslett was deeply concerned about a thumb deactivated through its lack of exercise. This seemed to vaguely support the ancient belief of all mothers that if we cross our eyes, they might get stuck that way. Perhaps there was hope for me. She created a daily five-minute regimen of strict thumb exercise.

Five minutes a day: that was my rehab. As kids gathered around my desk to watch, I'd bring my thumb out to limber up for its workout. I felt rather special, really; maybe I'd end up as an inspiring TV movie, though I still hoped for sci-fi.

When my mother heard about all this, her eyes grew extremely large, though they didn't get stuck that way. "*What* thumb exercises?" she asked. I quickly brought her up to speed and she began to laugh. Then she told me the actual truth—the story the rest of us had forgotten.

As a toddler, I had broken an orange juice glass and cut myself before Mom could pull me away. Indeed the scar is visible to this day. If Dad had looked closely and detected it, he might have remembered and wouldn't have had to improvise—not that he hadn't done a fine, creative job. I suspect he was a Show-and-Tell prodigy himself at one time.

There had been a quick trip to the doctor's office and a protective sock over my thumb for a time. But no one had realized that I'd severed a nerve. Consequently, when I picked up my first crayon, the right hand wasn't as efficient. I'm a natural righty, but it turns out that I've drawn all my cartoons and book illustrations over the years with my secondary paw.

The truth was much less exciting than my alien theory. Not only did the TV movie never happen, but I don't even get to use handicapped parking spaces. Besides, there are far stranger stops on the grand tour of my body. Here are some of the weird, unearthly powers I was born with:

- The ability to move my eyeballs back and forth independently of each other. Not only can I cross them, but also cross one while the other remains still.

- The ability to turn my feet around so they're facing the other direction. I'm very double-jointed.

- The ability to put both feet behind my head. Actually I've gradually lost this one over the years. I'm not as limber now, and adults find fewer uses for putting both feet behind their head. But I'll always have my memories.

Given these anatomical curiosities, I was a one-man Show and Tell. I never had to hunt for robins' nests or conch shells. Wouldn't you rather hear about mutant thumbs?

Today my bod is odder than ever. For example, my hair has organized itself into two dissenting groups: one is changing color and the other is abandoning ship.

My sinuses predict barometric pressure changes. Too bad I didn't become a certified meteorologist.

Portions of my body are lumpy and no longer in conformance with standard fashion design. I find myself buying clothing in stores with names like "Barnum's Bargain Outlet for Strangely Proportioned Men."

Going to bed at night now involves a complex arrangement by which my lower back, sore shoulders and trick elbow must find a position on which they can all agree. I now eat prescription pizza, and when the nurse puts me on the scales I place my thumbs in my ears and sing "Na na na na!" in a loud voice to avoid hearing the ugly results. Sometimes I have thoughts about getting in better shape, but I always lie down and rest until the thoughts go away.

And I'm resigned to learning more medical terms than I ever desired. Fuch's dystrophy is an eye problem that causes blurry vision. Within a year or two I'll be facing corneal implants in both eyes, as my present corneas are less and less capable of draining fluids.

My bod is decidedly odd. It may not have been much of a prize to begin with, but I miss it all the same. It never occurred to me that I would ever be in such need of a trade-in. It's not possible for now, but I cling to I Corinthians 15. In that passage Paul promises me that upgrades will indeed be available someday. There is mystery here, as there always is when the Bible touches on questions of eternity. Our minds simply cannot grasp the greater world that lies beyond this one, wider than space and more durable than time.

Paul suggests that these bodies of ours are nothing more than seeds planted for a future harvest. "When you sow, you do not plant the body that will be," he writes, "but just a seed, perhaps of wheat or of something else" (I Cor

15:37). The wheat seed is buried in the soil, cracks and awaits the miracle. A new and greater life springs from it, and the dead seed has achieved its purpose.

I understand the metaphor of "cracked seeds." And I wonder about the resurrection body waiting for me. I turn to Philippians 3:21, where Paul writes that Christ "will transform our lowly bodies so that they will be like his glorious body." When I was younger, such verses meant little to me; they were theological abstractions at best. As I grow older, I reflect upon them with deepened interest.

I look forward to inheriting such perfection. On what the old spiritual calls "that great gittin' up mornin'"; after I have been planted in the ground and sprinkled with the living water of eternity, I will rise to find that all the pain, decay and corruption of an old cracked seed has passed away.

How deep will my joy be? It's impossible to even imagine for now. I will be only one perfect, golden grain of wheat in a limitless field of them, blossoming toward the heavens and joining in a rustling chorus of praise and worship. I realize wheat is only a metaphor—little more than a crude symbol of something that will be glorious and eternally magnificent.

But so is this body, this odd and imperfect body, which

will have to do for now. I think I'm going to donate it for theological research after I'm gone. I know there are better things to come, and I give that a thumbs-up—with a perfect, bendable thumb.

2

THE MOTHER'S DAY GIFT

It is a summer day in 1959, hot and humid in the way that is inevitable when Atlanta and August collide. It's not difficult for me to imagine the whir of the electric fan and the laughter of four young women gathered around the card table; four girlfriends enjoying an afternoon of bridge. My mother, one of the three guests, cannot realize she will never again play this particular game. It's her final game of bridge.

I can almost hear the doorbell ring and see the surprise, then the anxiety, written in her eyes. She wonders why my father's face appears through the doorway. Why is he so grave, so pallid? What is he doing here in the middle of a workday?

He is here to bring the news that De'er, my maternal grandmother, is dead. On vacation, in a little gift shop in the Florida Keys, she has suffered a massive coronary and fallen amidst the racks of seashells and beach trinkets.

A few days later, my mother joins her father and two sisters for the funeral. My mother's short life has included no experience with death or funerals; she has no idea how to comfort herself, nor what to do with the tumult of emotions inside her. She wants to collapse into someone's arms, weep, and hear words of consolation. But her sisters, understandably enough, are busy ministering to their father's grief. As the sisters huddle together in one of the bedrooms, waiting for the funeral, one of them says to my mother, "Nancy, we are *not* going to cry at this service. Mother never liked any kind of public display of emotion. We will hold our heads up in a way that would have made her proud."

My mother has always been free with tears, and this additional burden is almost unbearable. But surely her sisters, both years older than her, know best. It is a lovely summer day, but as the procession leaves the church, the clouds suddenly open and the roofs of the cars are pounded with rain. Thunder-bursts shout their anger across the sky. It seems as if the heavens themselves are weeping the tears that my mother has been denied.

In the days that follow, she struggles to master herself, to rein in the chaos of her emotions. She was the baby—her mother's baby. The two of them talked on the phone nearly every day. She is 27, with two small boys. De'er has led her by the hand through every crisis of a young wife and mother. That reassuring voice has been stilled, even as the postcards continue to arrive—three cards mailed shortly before her death, perhaps one of them just outside that gift shop where my grandmother was taken from us.

My mother receives the cards one by one. "It is so hot here, and I feel so far away from home," De'er writes. My mother will cling to these postcards from heaven in a hand that no longer writes, from a comforter who will no longer counsel, to a daughter who can no longer run into her arms.

My mother now discovers she cannot swallow. Ever since the funeral, there has been a painful lump in her throat. A doctor will confirm she has been swallowing her grief.

In the evenings, she prays. She says to God, "Tell my mother that I'm all right and that I said hello." It sounds a little silly to her, a little immature. But it helps her cling to the truth that her beloved one is not really gone, but only in a better place. Nor does my mother hold God responsible. She only wishes he would send comforters. My father is a sympathetic and understanding listener—but who can replace one's mother?

My mom attends church and gazes at the sea of dispassionate faces around her. This is my father's church. She likes it here, enjoys Dr. Swilley's preaching, even considers joining the choir someday. But there are no shoulders of comfort here. Why should they pay much attention to her? She's not even a member. She is here so her boys will be in Sunday school, because that is how she has been raised. Her friends in the ladies' class are always nudging her to walk down the aisle, to be baptized, to become a member. But until today, this has not been about her. Until Mother's Day of 1960, it has always been about her husband and her boys.

Now, on a spring day after a long winter's mourning, she is all too conscious of the occasion. This is her first Mother's Day without a mother. The pews around her are filled with smiling faces, and why shouldn't they smile? Many of them are years, decades older than her, and they have their mothers. Their children have jolly, gracious grandmas to spoil them, to watch them grow, to help with the raising.

Still, my mother is grateful to be here. Worship is a safe haven, with its music and preaching and prayer. She is closer to God here, and therefore closer to her mother. The pastor speaks with eloquence of the great matriarchs of the Bible. How the words paint a picture of De'er; she would have liked this sermon.

But then there is the hymn of invitation, and a wave of emotion suddenly washes over my mother; an irresistible tug at her heart and her feet. She whispers briefly to her husband, slides clumsily toward the aisle, and walks rapidly to the front of the sanctuary. She is weeping uncontrollably, making a scene, and all the eyes of the sanctuary are fastened on her. But surely De'er wouldn't have been ashamed. This, after all, is for *her*. This is the final Mother's Day present, the only one my mother can still offer.

"You are my only child who has not been immersed," De'er had often said. It used to worry her so. Mom always smiled and changed the subject, but now she will fulfill her late mother's wish. She will give this gift, and somewhere in heaven, her mother will smile and nod.

My mother will join the church, receive the baptism, seek the comforters. Dr. Swilley greets her at the front of the sanctuary, but my mother can't slip a single intelligible word through the spasms of weeping. "It's all right. Sit over here," the pastor whispers as he delicately helps her toward a pew. Then the music has faded, and he is introducing Mrs. James W. Suggs Jr. as a new member. My father proudly joins her at the front, placing a reassuring arm around her shoulders.

Then there is a little surprise. While she has attended the church for several years, it hasn't occurred to her that baptism would be something immediate. They plan on doing it tonight! During the afternoon, she catalogues every conceivable excuse to postpone her appointment with the baptismal pool.

But this is a gift for her mother, and there can be no strings attached. So she consents. And that night, she feels the cool water caress her face. As she breaks the surface again, she thinks, "I have never felt this clean in my life." She looks out across the evening congregation and sees a sea of smiles—not strangers anymore, but friends and comforters.

Four decades somehow arrive and depart, leaving their marks and their lessons in all of us. My mother, in her seventieth year, looks out across that same congregation from the choir loft. She reflects on that long-ago Sunday when she offered her gift. She considers the many lessons of life and love that she has learned since then. Over four decades, she has journeyed deeply into the Scriptures. She has discovered the meaning of the lordship of Christ and the power of the Holy Spirit. She has shared her faith, involved herself in mission projects and ministered to scores of young couples, children and dozens of our friends. She has become a respected leader in the church.

Not only has my mother found comfort, but she also has become a comforter. She is a survivor of breast cancer and a bilateral mastectomy, and God has sent fearful young women across her path frequently, so that she could help them gently into the arms of "the God of all comfort, who comforts us in all our troubles, so that we can comfort those in any trouble with the comfort we ourselves have received from God" (2 Cor 1:3-4).

Now she looks out across a sea of brothers and sisters, and she whispers to herself, "Where else could I find a family such as this? Where else could I find such warmth? Where else could there be so many people whom I truly love, and who have loved me?"

And she reflects that once upon a time, when there was a tug at her heart on Mother's Day of 1960, she was not the giver of the gift, as she had thought. She was merely the recipient. Someday she will thank her mother in person.

Someday they will embrace once again, reunited forever. But until that day, her mother has helped her toward a foretaste of that glory: the motherhood of the church itself, with its plentiful wisdom, love and strong shoulders.

3

THE SUNDAY MORNING CHAMPION

On Sunday mornings, my brother Jim and I munched our breakfast cereal and stared at *Gospel Jubilee* on television. We had little choice; it was that or the Indian-head test pattern. Every week, just as we were trying to figure out which member of the male trio sang like a three-hundred-pound bullfrog (it was often the skinny fellow, actually), Mom would fall upon us with bow ties and checkered sports jackets. It was time to go see God and Grandmother, one for church and the other for dinner.

We argued about the bow ties, of course. I understood how God would like seeing us all cleaned up; but then again, why was it that none of the Bible characters seemed to wear choking bow ties? Most of them wore comfortable and loose-fitting bathrobes. Why couldn't we go to church like that? I never did receive a good answer to that question.

It was also hard to imagine cool figures such as Noah or Samson sitting through one of our worship services. The preacher talked about spending all of eternity praising God, but sixty minutes was enough of an eternity for me. If I got everlasting life, this bow tie and checkered sport jacket would be the death of me. And the idea of sitting up there somewhere listening to billion-year-long choral cantatas—no wonder people weren't rushing down the aisle to join up.

Mom and Dad wouldn't let us crawl under the pews, stare at the old people behind us or play board games. And in those days, if nature called, you didn't answer the phone. I imagined little monsters in the strange, twining, wine-colored pattern on the carpet. I counted the crystal pieces in the chandeliers. I drew gory war scenes all over the bulletin, with planes dive-bombing the Organ Prelude and Call To Worship.

I tried to listen; I really did. I knew God was watching my brother and me from overhead, probably using the chandelier as a magnifying glass to reveal every little act of misbehavior. And the pastor threw around words such as *sanctification, vicarious* and something that sounded like *Stuartship*— perhaps a church founded on the teachings of Stuart? It was all so bewildering; what I needed was the Worship Service Secret Decoder Ring.

At least we had Sunday school; I hoped eternity would be more like this place. We heard amazing Bible stories and made little missionary people out of Popsicle sticks. We sang "Jesus Loves the Little Children" and "This Is My Father's World." Then there was Memory Work, a lost art. We all had the King James Version, of course, and that was a good thing. When you memorized a verse out of the KJV, it stuck. I love our modern translations, but instead of "Be ye kind, one to another," we now have something like, "Be nice to folks." It's just not the same when it comes to Memory Work.

Those teachers could really motivate us, too. One of my big brother's teachers tossed handfuls of candy to kids who could recite verses—a Tootsie Roll for John 3:16, a Snickers bar for Proverbs 3:5. The word on the street was that if you could nail the entire book of Leviticus, you'd hit the mother lode. Maybe you'd have candy for *life* and wouldn't even want to go to heaven. Of course, when I reached that department, I got an insurance agent for a teacher.

Even without the chocolate, the basic competitive drive was enough to spur us on. We wanted to learn God's Word the fastest so we could lord it over the other kids in a Christian manner. A chart on the wall showed everyone's name and how many verses he or she had memorized. The teachers made it clear to us: if you were at the bottom of that chart, you were one sorry excuse for a Christian. If you, the Memory Work Cellar-Dweller, made it to heaven at all, St. Peter would probably snub you in public. No, those Bible characters were only going to hang out with the Memory Work Magnates, who learned thirty or forty verses during the quarter.

By that logic, in the next world the girls would be running everything. After all, they always finished the whole quarter's worth of verses in two weeks, then spent the rest of the time smirking and sticking out their tongues. Of the guys, only two or three of us struggled for the middle of the chart. I don't know why we couldn't keep up; maybe those bow ties cut off the circulation to the brain.

I can remember when the race among the boys came down to two of us. I attempted a sneaky end run to get my name to the top of the chart by memorizing the last seven or eight long passages—some of them entire psalms—in one weekend. Naturally my rival did exactly the same thing and we finished in a disappointing tie. What was the point of memorizing forty Bible passages just to tie?

Maybe the point was that after all these years, when thousands of facts from high school and college have trickled out the back of my brain somewhere, those King James verses are still with me. I may have never made the top of the chart, but I'm thankful from the bottom of my heart.

As for the teachers, some made a lasting impact and some never showed up. Some dully read straight from the quarterly; others never used the quarterly at all. Some of them let us talk about football for the whole period. I remember one of them scolding us for the day's attendance: "Only fifty-two percent of you here! If this were a test at school, you would have just *failed!*" We were told it was our Christian duty as fourth-graders to be scouring the hedges and the highways for lost souls. Yet somehow it was just The Chipster, Booger Williams and I who showed up every week.

Promotion Sunday always came in October. At that time

we would move up to the next grade and meet our new teachers. Only one Promotion Sunday sticks in my memory. That was the day my father and mother were introduced as adult workers for the fifth-grade department. It was hard for me to imagine my parents in a classroom with The Chipster or Booger Williams. What would it be like to hear my dad tell a Bible story?

My father was unlike any teacher I'd ever encountered. All the various facets of his personality—his sense of humor, his studiousness, his salesmanship—came together perfectly in his role as a Bible teacher. Dad was in his element sitting behind the little wooden table with his note cards. He prepared his lessons carefully and knew how to communicate with boys. He used examples and illustrations to bring the lessons to life. But looking back, I believe it was my father's passion for the material that really set him apart. He was clearly *excited* about what he was telling us, and we caught the fever. In my eyes, Dad was a Sunday morning champion—and I could follow behind him.

Dad and I had not bonded in the realm of sports, as he and my brother had. Before this moment, there had been no common interest to truly bring us together as father and son. But now, all of a sudden, of all places, we bonded in a fifth-grade Sunday school classroom. I had always loved the Bible stories. I was proud of my Dad, the consummate storyteller, and I wanted to be as much like him as possible.

By the time I was a teenager, Dad often called on me as a substitute teacher for his seventh-grade department. When I reached college, I was leading small Bible study groups. And today I can't be happy unless I'm teaching the Bible somewhere in some setting. For my career, I actually write about the Bible. What a difference it made that Dad awakened within me this passion for teaching the Scriptures.

Even today he's the best Sunday school teacher in his church. Generations of young Christians have been molded by his lessons, looking to both of my parents for advice and guidance. Many of these students have gone on to become teachers themselves.

Just last week, Dad shared with me his assignment to teach a lesson from Numbers. We laughed about the passage: slim pickings for a lesson! We had a great time looking at the verses together. This is still a special part of our relationship after thirty-five years. It's a bond that lingers, like the King James verses I hid in my heart so long ago.

These singular moments in life are like the monuments raised by the Israelites in order that they would know exactly where they were, who they were and how they got there, and in order that they would stop to thank God for the miracle. That Sunday in fifth grade was a monument in my life, and I return to it now and again for a moment of grateful worship. I lift it in celebration, just as it has lifted me.

4

THE HANDWRITING
ON THE WALL

Gym class was my least favorite event of the day, even on those occasions when I had a root canal scheduled. I couldn't climb the rope. I couldn't run the track. I couldn't play Massive Trauma Ball—or whatever was the name of that sport that involved being hunted down and ritually executed with a kickball.

Today, however, was particularly threatening. Old Coach was calling me by name. Once Old Coach knew your name, it meant you would never live to see the junior-senior prom.

I was sitting in the locker room, wringing out my rancid gym shorts, when it all happened. All in a moment, the familiar sounds of midpubescent laughter and towel snapping suddenly broke off. I looked up and there he stood in his smelly parka, framed by the fleeing columns of ninth-graders, who vanished like minnows in the wake of the shark. Old Coach towered before me, giving off that familiar coach-scent of mingled perspiration and Hai Karate aftershave, rattling his coach-keys and chewing on his silver whistle of death. His leg hairs rustled in the breeze of the fleeing kids.

"Suuuuggs," stated Old Coach, as if uttering a foul oath. "Hear yer an artist." As always, it was nearly impossible to understand his grunts and gravelese.

I looked to the right and to the left suspiciously. I always tried to achieve invisibility during this part of the day. For what terrifying purpose could Old Coach need me? He carried a clipboard and an enormous key-chain. For the first time it occurred to me to wonder which mysterious doors all those hundreds of keys opened. Dungeons perhaps? And how many pounds must those keys weigh altogether? I imagined he could quickly hurl them and decimate any kid who annoyed him.

Old Coach looked me up and down as he fingered those

keys. From a pocket of the smelly parka he produced a huge red Marks-A-Lot pen. "Mawn," he said, beckoning with a hairy finger. I interpreted this as "Come on" and followed obediently. Coach led me to the football stadium, where I instantly thought of Victory Trails and shuddered. Victory Trails were the ultimate punishment: sprints up and down the stadium steps.

To my relief, he was heading toward the press box. This was a tall, white, concrete box overlooking the gridiron. It had an iron ladder leading to its roof, and it was beside this ladder that we stopped.

"Suuuuuuuggs," he began, drawing out the word. He seemed to like the effect he could get with my name, like a lawn mower moving over a gravel bed. Old Coach wagged a thumb upward. "Wancha go up-top, write 'Lovett Spiders Only.'" He pointed vaguely to a spot fifteen feet up, on the white concrete. "Make it *big*. Make it *perfessional*."

Old Coach placed the pen in my somewhat trembling hand. But I hesitated in confusion. It's a little disorienting to follow orders that seem irrational. *Lovett*—that was our school. But our mascot wasn't the spider—we were the Lovett Lions. What could possibly be up with "Lovett Spiders Only"?

Then it occurred to me that I was dealing, after all, with Old Coach—he of the chainsaw tonsils. Maybe I'd simply heard him wrong. "Please, sir," I said, feeling like Oliver Twist asking for more gruel, "what, again, would you like me to write?"

"Yew heard me! *Lovett Spiders Only!*" He spat spectacularly on the pavement, and I watched to see if his spittle would eat through the cement.

Okay, this required some quick reasoning. Maybe I was dealing with obscure football terminology. That almost *had* to be the solution, didn't it? Then again, I liked football. I was familiar with most of the lingo, and I had never heard of any formation, position or tradition that had anything to do with spiders.

I tried one more time, in a desperate plea for clarification. "Lovett . . . Spiders . . . Only?" I whimpered.

"*Lovett Spiders ONLY!*" Old Coach was just about out of patience. He began crumpling metal keys in his left fist. Nothing involving those keys could possibly be a good sign. My back was to the wall, literally and figuratively. Nothing to it but to do it. I swallowed hard and began my journey up the ladder. At least I didn't have to climb a rope to get up there. Reaching the top and unsheathing the Marks-A-

Lot, I looked down at Coach one final time, swallowed hard, did what had to be done and did it to the best of my ability.

I lettered Coach's enigmatic message in stylish, one-foot-tall, red letters. Actually Old Coach was right about one thing: I was an artist, and my work was looking pretty good against that white paint. And I had a thought: If I truly pleased Old Coach, wouldn't he naturally want to show his gratitude? Perhaps I would be granted full amnesty from Victory Trails for a week. Maybe I would sit safely and watch other ninth-graders perish at Massive Trauma Ball.

My adrenaline was soaring by this time. On creative over-drive, I added a few flourishes to the red letters and topped off my message with an amusing cartoon spider. I had to admit I'd done an outstanding job. I still had no idea what the spider signified, but mine was not to question why; mine was just to do or to run Victory Trails.

Pleased with my work, I scurried down the ladder and smiled confidently as I handed Coach the pen. Now came the part where he would show his gratitude. Old Coach pocketed the Marks-A-Lot and grabbed the rungs of the ladder to climb up and survey my work, just as the Pope must have done for Michelangelo in the Sistine Chapel.

I was feeling much better. Maybe I wouldn't have to run

Victory Trails for the whole rest of the . . .

"Suuuuuuuuuuuuuuuuuuuggggs!"

The voice from above made my hair stand on end. Somehow it evoked both screeching tires and grinding metal.

"Ssssssuuuuuuuuuuuuuuuuuuuuuuuggggggs!"

It was the sound of a thousand sawmills run amuck; an outboard motor set to explode. I looked upward. A dirty blazer and tennis shoes were hurtling down the ladder, and I was directly in their path. I sprang clear at the last moment, the key-chain barely missing my head.

"I thought I told yew to write 'Lovett Spiders Only'!" Old Coach bellowed.

"I did, Coach, I did!" I blubbered in fear and confusion. "I wrote just what you told me, Coach!"

"You wrote 'Lovett Spiders'! I told you to write 'Lovett *Spiders*'! Do I gotta spell it out? S-P-O-T-T-E-R-S, *spiders!*"

The whole shocking truth soaked in. *Spotters.* As in football spotters. As in football spotters who sit atop press boxes, spotting whatever it is they spot for the coaches. And now there was a big, red, grinning spider in permanent ink with my name signed to it in red on our high school press box.

I was in quite a spot.

I remember wondering, as I made the final turn on my

sixty-seventh trip up the stadium steps, whether the Pope ever made Michelangelo run any Victory Trails.

Through my senior year I could walk by the press box and still see traces of my freshman iniquities. My sins were as scarlet Magic Marker, but now they were white as snow, thanks to several dozen coats of cheap whitewash. No matter how many times they painted over my work, you could still make it out. I believe Old Coach has since climbed the great gym rope to that heavenly stadium where the running tracks are paved with gold and St. Peter rattles his golden key as he makes the angels run Victory Trails.

It's easy to laugh about it now, but the Lovett Spiders incident actually foreshadowed my career destination. These days I still can't climb the rope, but I can edit book manuscripts. The Old Coaches of the world still come and find me. They say, "Hear yer an artist," and they hand me the Marks-A-Lot. I then attempt to take whatever it is they want to say and write it brightly and artfully where the whole world can read it—only on a computer instead of a wall.

And yes, I still experience a few "spiders"—those times when I think I heard what I believe you understand what you were attempting to say, but you failed to understand what I thought you were hearing when I attempted to say what I thought I understood what you were attempting to say.

As it says in the gospel of Luke—or actually in the film *Cool Hand Luke:* "What we have here is a failure to communicate." As a writer and editor, I do my best to "be quick to hear, slow to speak and slow to use permanent ink." Okay, that one's not actually in the Bible either. But I do spend a good deal of time trying to listen, not only at the office but also at home. I try to speak clearly to my children and listen well, as I send them up the ladder of life to make their own mark.

A BUMP IN THE ROAD

When she was sixteen, the doctors told my Aunt Kathy that half her life was over. They couldn't promise her much hope of living past thirty.

Kathy had come down with a mysterious illness, and my grandparents had finally traveled with her to Johns Hopkins in Baltimore in hopes of identifying the mystery illness. Kathy was diagnosed with systemic lupus erythematosus, a wide-ranging disorder of the immune system.

This was 1962, and girls of Kathy's age dreamed about the prom while she confronted issues of mortality. It was during that same period, and after being treated at Kathy's hometown hospital in Atlanta, that author Flannery O'Connor succumbed to lupus.

But somehow my aunt lived on—and how she did live. How do you approach life when, far too young, you've gazed into the eyes of death? Kathy's solution was to reject morbidity in favor of sheer *carpe diem* joy.

Health was a challenge she subdued, and for many years her body cooperated. The lupus life is one of remission and relapse, remission and relapse. Symptoms could disappear for months or years, only to leap back into her life with the lupine snarl of the wolf that gives the disease its name. She had her moments of despair, of course, but she never lost her resolve, never unfurled the white flag of surrender.

In the generous seasons of remission, Kathy redeemed the brief daylight for all that she could. There was a sense of urgency, of taking no day or breath for granted—but an unfettered joy, too. No one could open a birthday or Christmas present like Kathy. "Fabulous!" she would scream, throwing wrapping paper across the room. "I *had* to have it!"

Kathy survived to unwrap those presents on her thirtieth birthday, then her fortieth, even her fiftieth. After a while, the miracle was something we all took for granted. The rumors of her early demise had been somewhat exaggerated, and Kathy most likely outlived the doctors who had stroked their chins pessimistically in 1962.

Yet the Johns Hopkins experience had left its imprint on my aunt. In Baltimore she had seen the importance of attentive, capable and compassionate caregivers. In the ashes of her prognosis lay the spark of her hope; Kathy committed herself to teaching nurses. In time she became a widely honored nursing professor, the first in our state to hold a doctorate in her field. She became friend and mentor to thousands of students.

Kathy spoke little of these accomplishments when our family gathered for birthdays. She was too busy focusing on us. Kathy, though an aunt, was in essence the big sister we four brothers never had. She was only a few years older, and in the sixties, then the seventies, she liked the same records and movies we did. It was Kathy who took us to our first rock concerts and invited us to meet her exotic menagerie of friends. She had lived in San Francisco as a medical student, had witnessed the revolution and was the only person we knew in Atlanta who actually used the word *groovy*.

It was Kathy, too, whose apartment provided a shelter for nephews caught up in teenage crises. We knew that when one of us hit some bump in the road, sooner or later the phone was going to ring. "Okay now," Dr. Kathy would say, all business, "what's the deal?" And for several hours, we would pour it all out—arguments at home, problems at school. Kathy had a way of listening quietly for just the right amount of time before demanding, "So. What are you gonna do about this?" She was a world-class listener.

Then, after seasons of peace and accomplishment and blue skies, her lupus would flare up yet again. Several times she lay in the hospital fighting for her life. Every nurse in the building knew and loved her, of course, so she received all kinds of extra care. But her family loved her the best. When Aunt Kathy needed a kidney, it was my brother Jim who stepped forward to donate it. His courageous sacrifice bought her a few more months, perhaps a few more years. Kathy was grateful and so were we, though we knew that even this gift would provide no long term miracles.

If only we could have given her even more; if only we could have donated months and years. There would have been donors lined up all the way to the West Coast. But there was only one possible outcome, and we all knew it. She beat the medical odds over and over, but in time she came up one miracle short.

In the days following my aunt's funeral we gathered to

laugh and cry over the Kathy stories, many of which had reached legendary status. Reliving them, after all, was one way to make her live again. No matter how well we know someone, they retreat into shadows of mystery when we lose them. We're struck by questions we can never ask them. We forget the tilt of the head and the cadence of the step. Who was this person? What were her secrets? What were her dreams?

Then we remember some trifling story or mannerism, and her laughter echoes again; we can almost hear her footsteps in the hall. The little stories and slices of life preserve the soul better than any Kodachrome print. Kathy was at the center of so many stories, but there is one that somehow captures her best.

Kathy was coming home very late after a really good party. It was about four o'clock in the morning and she was tired. Suddenly, as she cruised through a suburb, she felt a sickening thump under the car's wheels. She had barely seen the little animal in her headlights, but there was no doubt she'd run it over. Kathy, with her great nursing heart, was horrified.

She pulled to the side of the road and bundled the little creature into her coat. Crying a little, she walked up to the nearest door and rang the bell. In the middle of the night, it took a great while for a light to blink on behind the curtain. The man who came to the door had pillow-hair and one foot in slumberland.

Kathy stammered, "I'm sorry to wake you, but is this your dog?" She opened the coat and showed the man. He quickly gave her a piercing glare and slammed the door in her face.

Kathy moved on to the next home; surely someone could identify the little pet. But she received only another stare of angry disbelief and another slammed door.

As the morning light finally began to seep through the trees, Kathy walked into an animal hospital that was just opening for the day. The veterinarian, nursing his morning coffee, agreed to take a look. "I hit him accidentally, coming from a party," Kathy said. "I can't find his owner, and I don't know what to do."

The vet scrutinized the unfortunate creature for a moment and gently looked up at my aunt. "You've got a good heart, ma'am," he said. "But it seems like a lot of trouble to go to for a dead possum."

That was Kathy, always on her way to or from some celebration, hitting a bump in the road; Kathy, the wounded healer, going to great lengths to care for friends and strangers; and Kathy, somehow making us all laugh, even in the context of death. Her own life was reminiscent of Emily Dickinson's words: Because she could not stop for death, it finally stopped for her.

In the wake of losing her, I have thought a great deal about the lessons I need to learn from Kathy's life. Like every other human being, I live under a death sentence. What will I do with the brief daylight? I wish I had told Kathy how much she meant to me. I wish I had loved her better and given her more of the gift of my time. All I can do is try my best to live as she lived, to seize the day with joy and heal the hurting who come across my path.

Kathy spent a short lifetime tending the wounded: a friend with AIDS, a very young widow, a friend who was deeply depressed. I have learned that when God finds a willing doctor, he sends patients. Kathy's waiting room was always filled. Jesus, the original wounded healer, said that the rain falls on us all—the just and the unjust; the healthy and the afflicted; the patients and the caregivers. What finally sets us apart is that mysterious flame of the soul inside us, our ability to tend its fire and keep it burning as the storm rages; our determination not to horde the light, but to share it with the flickering candles around us.

My aunt's light was far too quickly extinguished. But it shines still in the glow of everyone whose life touched hers. And I trust that in the land she now calls home, there is eternal daylight and the ring of her laughter down every corridor.

6

LEAVE THE DRIVING TO US

My older brother was mentally prepared to operate a car by the time he was six. He leaned over the front seat, watched the driver carefully and memorized every move.

Not me. I was busy squatting down in the back seat and turning various shades of purple. It wasn't a good idea to take me for a ride if I had eaten a meal in the last several days. I christened most of Dad's new cars on their way out of the showroom, effectively removing that new-car smell. "Pull over," Mom would bellow at my Dad. "Fire in the hole!"

Dad had quick reflexes, but never quite quick enough.

At fifteen I received my learner's license, but I was in no

particular hurry to break it in. My idea was to take my time and let the real know-how of driving seep in by osmosis. Therefore I was mildly annoyed to discover Driver Education in the tenth-grade curriculum at school. I had thought Driver Ed was an actual person. But no, Old Coach taught the class in his patented umpire-like grunts. Because there was no language course offered in Conversational Old Coach, no one had the faintest idea what he was saying during his lectures; we depended heavily on audiovisuals and body language.

Then came the day I found my name on the class driving schedule. A decree went out from Old Coach that I would be taking the car for a spin under his able guidance. At this point I had still never driven and had no idea where to begin. I might as well have been piloting the Apollo XI Lunar Excursion Module. It occurred to me I had better find out what that dashboard thing was all about. And those pedals on the floor—what was up with them?

So the night before my maiden voyage, I climbed into the family car and briefly studied the controls. Oh, my. There were more clutches, knobs and buttons than I had realized. For example, could this prominent thingie be the car's "on" button? *Ouch!* It was apparently a cigarette lighter. Okay, that was helpful; I was making progress already.

I was vaguely certain that a pedal was used to stop the vehicle, and yet another to move it forward. That struck me as confusing. The textbook said the one on the right propelled the car forward—an important pedal, and one I would endeavor to recall.

So far, it was clear that my bicycle skills weren't going to help me. Still, I had made a B in trigonometry; how much harder could this be?

The next day I took my place behind the wheel in the school's durable old driver's ed sedan. Old Coach sat on the passenger side with his clipboard, rattling his coach-keys. Student Driver #2 sat in the back, the on-deck hitter. Coach grunted something that seemed to carry the connotation of "Play ball!" I hesitated a moment, then reached for a knob. "This is the cigarette lighter," I noted. "Just so you know."

Coach grunted again with the connotation of impatience, so I closed my eyes, gulped and turned the key. The engine roared into action. Hey, I was good at this! A little touch of confidence surged through my veins.

Next it stood to reason that I should back the car out of its parking place. So I hunted down the slot marked R, thrust the knob there and mashed the floor pedal completely to the floor according to the formula I had memorized.

When the dust cleared, the car had magically stopped, over on the other side of the road, several inches from a steep embankment. I saw that Old Coach had elected to use the instructor's emergency brake. As a matter of fact, he was now wrapped bodily around the instructor's emergency brake and trembling feverishly. The sun through the windshield reflected on a few of his former hairs gently floating down from the ceiling. The kid in the back let out a long, low whistle. *"Dang,* Suggs," he said with admiration.

Out the window, I saw several ninth-graders running for cover.

"Suggs." It was Old Coach's voice, coming from beneath the glove compartment, muffled but calm. "This your first time?"

"Sir, no *sir,* Coach!" I replied indignantly. "Well, sort of, sir. I studied a bit last night."

Old Coach eventually got disentangled and arranged himself once more in the passenger seat. But there was a furtive, hunted-animal look in his eyes now. We headed out the school's back gate very, very slowly. Old Coach had suggested we try a little game that involves moving the car at speeds slower than three miles per hour. The road had deep embankments sharply dropping off on each side, and it was here that I learned some important points on steering. *"Left*leftleftleft—*Suuuuuggs!"* my instructor screamed as we narrowly averted plunging through the barbed wire and into the forest. The kid in the back seat was hollering and lifting his arms as if on a roller coaster.

Old Coach was certainly helpful the rest of the session. With his hands clamped firmly over mine on the steering wheel, his foot could just barely reach the instructor's brake, but he managed it. I was disappointed when he came down with a rare disease on the day of my next turn behind the wheel. The time after that, he had a relapse.

Eventually my father was resigned to giving me driving lessons. I think Mom was considered exempt because in the event of a driving lesson catastrophe, the family would have no one to cook or do laundry. And the life insurance policy was in Dad's name. Well, I felt I was making progress, but after the second trip, when Dad fell trembling and moaning from the passenger door, he made a phone call. Dad had decided his life was valuable, too—he called his younger brother and made some kind of pact they still won't discuss.

Uncle David took me out on Sunday afternoons, and he actually held up rather well. I have a lot of happy memories about those Sundays learning how to drive. Uncle David was very calm and methodical. Then Aunt Kathy took me for a spin or two. Before my father actually got to bargaining with third cousins or traveling gypsies, I had actually learned how to drive a car.

Looking back, I wonder how my parents survived that ordeal. I guess that's simply what families do. At appropriate intervals we teach our kids to drive, to handle money, to go on dates, to navigate all the sharp curves and treacherous embankments of growing up. We can put our hands over theirs and guide the wheel at first. But the day comes when that instructor's brake is taken away, and we have to let them drive away on their own.

Solomon, the wise king, has no driver's ed pointers in the book of advice he wrote for his son—but he comes close. The author speaks of following the path, of staying on the safe road. "Do not forget my words or swerve from them," he says in Proverbs 4:5. "Let your eyes look straight ahead, fix your gaze directly before you," says driving instructor Solomon a few verses later in verse 25.

Parents understand. Our mother worried herself sick each and every evening we went out with our friends as teenagers. Didn't she trust us? I think she did; it was the rest of the world that deeply concerned her. If we came in late, she was always waiting in the kitchen with these particular words, never varying: "I thought you were in a ditch somewhere!"

There were actually very few ditches between our house and the mall, the school, the church or any of the places we drove. What ditch did she have in mind? We had a good laugh and kidded her endlessly about the hazards of ditches teeming with unwary teenagers who hadn't listened to their mothers.

Yet it wasn't long before my brother Steve, seven years my junior, got his driver's license and had his first date on the same evening. I didn't like the idea of my baby brother operating a powerful automobile and figuring out the mysteries of courting at the same time. I wondered if he knew where the cigarette lighter was in a car. Sometime after midnight I wandered into the kitchen, fixed a cup of coffee and joined my mom at the breakfast table. "Welcome," said Mom.

"Tell me again about the ditches," I said.

Now I have two kids of my own, and I'm wrapped around that instructor's brake about as tightly as a father could be. I tell my kids, "Leave the driving to us." But I know the truth: love requires the pain of letting go. At some point, Mom and Dad trusted us enough to hand us the car keys after sundown. I took it completely for granted at the time, but now I see it as a courageous act of faith and love. What an agonizing moment for a parent. Did God feel something similar when he handed Adam and Eve the keys to the garden?

He knew what we strain to remember: that there is no love without the sacrifices demanded by trust; that the deepest joy in life is seeing the child come home, freely returning the love we have liberated.

None of which forbids me from cheating with a few early driving lessons for my two children. "Look straight ahead," I tell them on the way to Burger World. "Fix your gaze directly before you. And remember, this here is the cigarette lighter. Solomon said that; you could look it up."

LOVE AT FIRST FLIGHT

Love is a word, but marriage is a sentence.

At least that was my story in 1986, and I was sticking to it. Maybe marriage was a fine institution, but who said I belonged in an institution? So on the day I first met Gayle, hearts and flowers were not on my agenda. It was perfect timing, in other words, for one of Cupid's drive-by shootings.

We first met at a Sunday afternoon planning session at church. Six single adults were planning to visit Wiesbaden, West Germany, to speak at a conference primarily for American soldiers stationed in that region. We would also consult with a few English-speaking churches on the subject of ministering to single adults. Then there would be several days for sightseeing.

I already knew four of the other five team members—all but one named Gayle Bailey. As I would soon find out, Gayle excels at grand entrances. She exploded into the room several minutes late, dressed in red and talking faster than my ears could follow. My first impression was that she was more a force of nature than a Baptist missionary.

Her first impression of me was that of a somber scholarly type who probably seldom laughed and was likely to have little patience with red-garbed forces of nature.

Over the weeks, we eyed each other suspiciously while fine-tuning our seminar materials. Then, on Easter Sunday, the six of us met at the Atlanta airport, ready for international adventure—*discrete* international adventure. We were well aware that only a week earlier, the United States had bombed Libya in response to the terrorism of Muammar al-Qaddafi. The Atlanta Symphony Chorus had cancelled a trip to France, and many tourists were staying home. After some discussion, we had decided to stay the course. We were a small group, capable of traveling quietly. The key was to be discrete.

I could imagine the other team members moving discretely through international airports; I wasn't too certain about Gayle, who always seemed as if she'd had five or six cups of coffee—in a *good* way, I hasten to add as she looks over my shoulder and reads this paragraph.

Gayle seemed capable of holding forth on any given subject for hours. And I was fascinated by how she never left a story unfinished, no matter what. She might be talking about, say, her third cousin's red tractor. Some sudden interruption might intervene—say, a meteor might crash into the earth several feet away. Panic might break out all around us. Everyone in sight of the meteor might be quarantined for a week. CNN might arrive to do interviews. Then, after CNN left, Gayle was certain to say, "So anyway, as I was saying about my third cousin's red tractor . . ."

I learned some of these delightful idiosyncrasies on the long flight to Frankfurt. Sitting next to Gayle made the hours pass quickly. We talked about our books. We talked about our jobs. We talked about the shortcomings of the in-flight movie. It may not have been love at first sight, but it was something very close to love at first flight, at least from my seat. By the time we wearily made our way through West German customs—*discretely*—it was as if we had known each other all our lives.

A busy seven days of seminars, church visits and consultations came and went. Then, during the second week, we were free to explore the blue mountains and Black Forest of Bavaria. The six of us traveled across the lovely countryside by train, staying in cheap *pensions* by night and deciding where to visit when we rose the next morning. We had the time of our lives. I truly believe my feelings for Gayle would have grown the same if we had been trudging through the Sahara Desert. But we certainly were not. Castles on the Rhine and mist-shrouded cathedrals are powerful romantic stimulants.

By the time the two of us were strolling outside King Ludwig's royal Bavarian castle, Neuschwanstein, I no longer seemed somber or scholarly; goofy and google-eyed would be better adjectives. As we strolled in the lovely evening, we saw a breathtaking vision. Mountain mist was rising into the night air, and the well-lit castle seemed to float in the evening sky on a cloud bed, with no ground beneath it.

If I had known Gayle for more than a few days, what better moment could there have been to pop the question? But darn it, we hadn't even been on a date, and somehow, "Dearest Gayle, would you be in my Bible study group?" didn't have the right ring to it.

A few days later we were back in Atlanta, reshackled to our respective jobs. I kept in touch with Gayle over the phone. We had dinner together once, but things seemed different between us now. Clearly Gayle liked spending time with me, and the chemistry was still there. But she seemed more reserved than she had been overseas, and nary a floating castle in sight.

Finally I coaxed the truth out of her. I was crestfallen to discover that some hideous, heinous, loathsome male person had gotten there before me. In short, Gayle had a boyfriend.

In the past I would have given up immediately. But this time I was stubborn; I fought the good fight, refusing to turn away from Gayle. I wrote her letters. I kept up with her on the phone. But most of all, I prayed.

Never had I prayed so passionately about one particular issue. I knew this was a crucial turning point for me and that God cared about my feelings. I kept a journal of my prayer during this time, and I sought God day and night. I offered all the usual pious phrases, but my raw, honest emotions always crept in. "Thy will be done in this relationship, and may I accept thy loving plans as the wisest counsel for my life," I prayed humbly. "But *please please please* make Gayle dump that phony charlatan right now! C'mon, Lord, you know that clown is wrong for her! Can't you smite him or something? But hey, thy will be done, whatever."

What really rankled me was that my rival had an unfair advantage. Gayle worked with him during the day. So I gave the Lord a piece of my mind on that account, too. "Lord, it isn't fair!" I whined. "She knows I'm better for her, but how can she break off that relationship when she sees him eight hours a day?"

The day after I prayed this, two eye-opening events occurred. First Gayle called to say that her company had gone bankrupt. Everyone, including her, was out of a job. Then, not long after I put down the phone, our secretary came to me and told me she would be taking medical leave for three weeks. She pointed out that we would need a temporary replacement. Did I know anyone who needed a short-term job?

Good one, Lord!

I knew God didn't cause a small company to go bankrupt just to supply my romantic needs. Still . . . one had to wonder. If God wanted to work in mysterious ways, that was fine by me.

I called Gayle and told her there was a three-week job available to help her pay the bills while she was looking for a permanent position. And within a few days, I was the one with eight-hours-a-day lobbying access. In time Gayle made the decision to break off the former relationship, which she realized was not best for her.

I had long since understood that there was no one in the world I could love any more, no one who could be such a perfect soul mate. Gayle came to her senses. I had told her about my amazing prayer life, and she was worried that if she didn't marry me, I might pray again and she could end up working for me *permanently*.

The following spring we made the German mission trip for the second time, but on this occasion it was our honeymoon. The castles were just as misty, the cathedrals just as atmospheric, but we needed no floating castles. The way God had brought us together and the way we fit together were much more miraculous. After sixteen years of marriage, it seems even more so. Of God's many wonderful gifts to me, none has so richly, so deeply blessed my life. I have no idea where I would be today, or what kind of person I would be, if God had not sent Gayle across my path.

The two of us have a marital commitment that is more entrenched than any castle. We have a spiritual foundation more glorious than any cathedral. The Lord is the architect of this union, and he has knit our souls together with the fibers of a love whose source can only be heaven.

As I look back on that first meeting, Gayle was not a force of nature after all, but an act of God. We both dread that moment when the limits of mortality will separate us. Even so, I can imagine arriving in heaven, that ultimate palace floating on the clouds, and searching everywhere for Gayle. Somewhere I'll find her, we'll embrace, and she'll say, "So, anyway—about the tractor . . ."

8

CHIP OFF THE OLD BLOCKS

Ole Kirk Christiansen was a master carpenter from Billund, Denmark. He assembled furniture and, when he had time, the occasional wooden toy for his children. His twelve-year-old son worked with him in the shop.

One day the two of them stumbled across an idea for constructing children's building blocks that fit snugly together by the use of small pegs and holes—blocks that really connected and weren't easily toppled.

Christiansen decided to market his little idea. He needed a name, so he pegged together the Danish words for "play" and "well." The result was the name LEGO. It was only years later that someone told him that *lego* was also Latin for "I build."

Within a few years, LEGO blocks were a best-selling product. The Christiansen legacy is an icon, a toy empire. And the whole enterprise was built on two powerful ideas: the simple gratification of a firm connection and the human impulse to build.

I became an expert on LEGOs—not that I had any choice in the matter. Our five-year-old son was the Frank Lloyd Wright of peggable plastic. As I came home exhausted from work, Robert would greet me with "C'mon, Daddy! We have to build!"

And so we built. We played well. LEGOs provided a way for my son and me to peg together, to forge a tight connection for a few hours.

Robert set out one day to construct the ultimate plastic tower. It would be his most ambitious project, his masterwork of the building-block medium. It wasn't long before I had gotten myself involved, giving advice and demonstrating a few tricks to tighten up the structure. A brick should have multiple connections, I pointed out, rather than pegged exclusively to the one beneath it. Multiple connections provide stability.

Soon we were adding tall windows and ledges. We rationed our block supply, carefully figuring how tall our tower could possibly climb. We measured out our LEGOs by shape and color. Would we reach the ceiling? Would the building stand without swaying?

The sky was the limit, or at least the ceiling; so was that other unbreachable boundary, Robert's bedtime. I'd whine more about it to his mom than Robert did. Yet my son granted solemn permission for me to boldly continue our quest without him. "Daddy, you can play while I'm asleep," he'd say. I'd blush and stammer for him to get on to bed. I'd share a Bible story, listen to prayers and kiss my two children goodnight.

Then, when I could hear Robert breathing regularly . . . I'd play LEGOs. Maybe just another brick or two; maybe I could strengthen this flying buttress over here. The deadly tendrils of obsession were getting their grip on me. My wife even got into the act. We found ourselves sitting there on the corner of the family-room floor scuffling over the last red three-pegger. "Let me have that and I'll clean the toilet for the next three weeks," I said, perspiration dampening my brow. Gayle only cackled and closed her fist on my brick.

When I was growing up, it was jigsaw puzzles. We would

compete to scoop up the edge pieces, the easy connections. And there was always a nerve-racking race to see who got to insert that last satisfying piece. I realized that, then as now, it wasn't so much about interlocking the pieces as interlocking the people. Families, too, need those tight, sturdy connections.

One morning at breakfast I was eager for Robert to see the progress of his tower. I had been as industrious as the shoemaker's elves. Our skyscraper topped off at a height of nearly six feet and featured a balcony with an arched arcade and ornamental balustrades. It was the Trump Tower of Candyland.

"Take a look, Robert!" I said. "Whaddaya think?"

To my astonishment, Robert wasn't smiling. He was pale. "Daddy, you needed me to help you!" he said, on the verge of tears. He reached for the pinnacle, but the plastic skyscraper now transcended his grasp.

This had all begun as his own little project, and now he couldn't even add a block. "You needed me to help you," he repeated through his tears.

I was speechless. Why hadn't I caught myself in my excess of zeal? I had ruined everything. It took some coaxing, but I won my son back to the project. There was a way we could still finish the building together, but it took some lobbying before the zoning board: Gayle waived the regulations that kept Robert from standing on the sofa, and we carefully moved the tower beside it. Soon the budding builder was happily laying bricks on the top floors, and he and I were reconnected.

The bricks ran out as we approached the ceiling. Sitting on my shoulders, Robert, with a huge grin, crowned the spire with a tiny flag. Gayle snapped our picture and captured the happy moment for posterity.

The imposing tower dominated our home for all of two proud days, the focal point of our house. No canvas by Picasso or Van Gogh could have been more happily savored. The thing would probably still be there if we hadn't placed it in a high-traffic neighborhood—right beside the doorway to the hall. Robert had to use the restroom, and time was of the essence. He shot by the proud plastic edifice a bit carelessly, brushing by like the second coming of Godzilla. The bricks of Babel II exploded and hurtled through the air, landing in every corner of the family room. We still pick them out of potted plants and from beneath sofa cushions to this day.

It had only required one reckless moment, and the dead

hulk of the tower's base lay sprawled across the rug—the death of a dream, toppled by the call of nature. Robert was actually philosophical about this sudden development. Maybe he knew there would be other days and other towers. Maybe he comprehended that when a little boy has to go, he has to go. Maybe he was simply subdued because this was the first time he'd ever seen his dad sobbing and pounding the floor with his fists.

On the other hand, there are connections more durable than plastic. We never realize the scope of the memories and traditions we're building when we take the time to play well together, to build. The LEGO website tells us that two eight-stud bricks can be fit together in twenty-four different ways; that three of the same bricks will fit together in 1,060 different ways. But six eight-stud bricks offer 102,981,500 unique ways of connecting.

Yet people can connect in many more ways than plastic. Gayle and I seek ever-new connections with our children. How can we "click"? Gayle works on Cub Scout projects with Robert. I help Sally with an art idea. Robert and I work on the proper techniques for throwing a baseball. Gayle teaches Sally about music.

The more connections we forge, the stronger the walls we

construct and the higher our family tower will climb. Ole Christiansen never realized that his little plastic blocks might forge connections far more durable than plastic in the generations that followed his own—generations when communities of all kinds were not strengthening but becoming disconnected.

I find it intriguing that Jesus, Peter and Paul all used the word picture of tower building. My favorite instance is found in Ephesians 2, in which Paul discusses the great "wall of hostility" that Christ has torn down, and the amazing spire of light that rises from the rubble. According to that epistle, Christ has erected a tower of unity—the anti-Babel—that reaches toward heaven. That first tower from Genesis ended in chaos when the builders could no longer speak and listen to one another. But Christ has accomplished precisely the opposite through this new, invisible tower that absorbs us into its gleaming magnificence and makes us one.

The cornerstone, Paul tells us, is Christ. The foundation is made up of prophets and apostles—the Old and New Testaments. And from that base, a tower made of human bricks "rises to become a holy temple in the Lord" (Eph 2:21). The Spirit of God supernaturally inhabits the tower we have become. I find that idea breathtaking. While Paul is speaking of the church, the same principle holds true for the holy assembly of a family.

"In him you too are being built together," according to the final verse of Ephesians 2. I want to be "built together" with my family in such a way that the Spirit of God comes to indwell the very bricks that connect us. To that end, we build. We play. We aim for the sky and look to the future.

Our building blocks may give out, but our spiritual architecture may rise until it touches heaven itself.

9

A BIRTHDAY SURPRISE

My daughter Sally has yet to make the transition from Barbie and balloons to boys and body piercing. For that I'm immensely grateful.

Sally still watches cartoons, holds hands with her parents and creates fantasy worlds for Chico, her hamster. Her grade-school friends are already talking about boyfriends and pop groups, but I'm thankful that Sally is squeezing every bit of joy and celebration out of childhood innocence that she can. I'm certainly in no hurry for her to grow up, because I've enjoyed her childhood as much as she has.

Well, most of the time. There *was* the matter of her eighth birthday.

We had a big party planned for her that Saturday. Of course, these days it isn't your father's birthday party. Cowboy Bob no longer comes to your house to do lasso tricks. No, today you must shuttle your kids to specialized birthday boutiques. Your little boy can take his comrades to a pint-sized racetrack, for example, and pilot miniature NASCAR vehicles at high speeds. Or you can take your kids to a miniature indoor amusement park, as we were doing.

As we entered the emporium, my senses were bombarded by what was clearly the Disney adaptation of Dante's Ninth Circle of Hell. Here were giant psychedelic pipes to crawl through, sliding boards to plummet down, video arcades and plenty of sugary cake and candy to ensure a frenzied experience for the children. I was overcome by sensory overload within seconds. Within minutes I began to weep and have flashbacks from Vietnam. And I've never been to Vietnam.

In every corner of the colossal room, kids were running rampant in a scene reminiscent of gang warfare in Candyland. And the sound was deafening. I decided that the best strategy was to stay close to the wall at all times, better to ward off assaults on my kneecaps. But I quickly found that floors, walls, chairs and tables were all adhering to me due to melted candy and cake icing that probably hadn't been hosed off for months.

Then my heart surged with hope: I discovered a room marked Men. I made a break for it as incoming cake shrapnel just missed me.

Maybe—just maybe—I would find inside this room a support group of shell-shocked dads huddling together for safety and listening to a soothing Mozart string quartet. Maybe then I could make it through the afternoon with sound mind and body. But no such luck; this was only a plain rest room. At least I could hide in here for the next three hours or so. Sanctuary! Not even Gayle would dare to enter a public men's room to drag me out.

An afternoon could move like molasses in a birthday emporium, yet Sally's first eight years had sped by all too quickly. In these quieter confines, I began to reflect on those ninety-six months. Where had they all gone?

Sally arrived on a chaotic day in 1991, a roller coaster experience that no birthday boutique could match. We had settled into bed the previous evening and turned out the light. At about one o'clock Gayle told me her time had arrived.

Sally was our first child. Even when life follows the script, the arrival of the first child is unique, unpredictable and unforgettable. Not that this occasion followed any script.

We threw on our clothes immediately and rushed to the hospital. It would be more than sixteen hours before Sally finally opened her eyes on this world.

We lost any sense of time as Gayle labored to bring us the child. There were prayers, hand holding, doctors checking in and out, more prayers, more hand holding and everything but the baby. I left for a quick breakfast, then a quick lunch hours later, fighting discouragement and first-time-daddy anxiety. My mother found herself comforting me as much as her daughter-in-law.

In my experience Sally has always been a dawdler. I think her name means "Hold on, I'll be there in a minute!" This was only the beginning. She was trying to emerge, the doctors told us, but her little body just couldn't make that first great journey. There came a terrible moment during the afternoon, during all the pushing and straining, when our daughter's tiny heartbeat disappeared momentarily from the monitor. Of course we didn't tell Gayle. But I know she saw the wild fear in my eyes.

I prayed frantically, angrily. My own heart missed a beat or two, and there was absolutely no hesitation on our part when the doctor suggested a cesarean section.

We moved from our cheerful, sky-blue delivery room to a severe white surgery unit buzzing with doctors and nurses. The Lamaze classes hadn't prepared us for this eventuality. I sat at the head of Gayle's bed and held her hand. A partition with curtains was placed across her chest to block us from viewing the details of the surgery.

I was an emotional wreck. Gayle, on the other hand, was treating the whole thing like a day-trip to the beach. At the moment, she was chatting up the doctors. "Which internal organs can you see?" she was asking them to my horror. This was more information than I needed or thought she needed at the moment—but it was her body, after all. She caught my astonishment and explained, "Well, I'm curious!" That's Gayle.

The moment came when I heard the most breathtaking of all sounds in this life—the first cries of our child. A moment later I was holding Sally's tiny, pink body. No words, of course, can encompass such a moment. Our firstborn was whole and healthy. She'd decided to join us in the outside world after all. I was already studying the eyes, the nose and the tiny mouth, checking for family resemblances. It has been observed that all newborns actually resemble Winston

Churchill, but don't tell that to a new father. I was speechless with awe and wonder.

And that's when it happened—the strangest, most unlikely of all reactions. At that euphoric moment, I experienced what I can only describe as a thunderous epiphany. I describe it to you at the risk of sounding contrived, of reducing life's most wonderful experience to an object lesson. Nothing could be further from my intent.

The truth is that at this of all moments, a single thought flashed through my mind and changed my understanding of God forever. Why would such a thought suddenly thrust up to the surface right then, while I was soaring on adrenaline, emotionally overcome by my first child?

Up to that moment, I had honestly never understood why God would love his human children to the degree the Bible assures us. I accepted the idea of "God-so-loved-the-world" in a dry, pedantic sort of way; I simply didn't feel it with any real passion. God is perfect, eternal, omnipotent; we are so weak, imperfect—vapors that linger for a moment and vanish. God should love me no more than I could love a snail. Not to mention that there are billions of us to love.

We who seldom achieve one single truly selfless moment; we who take all that God gives with both hands, then turn away in forgetfulness and ingratitude; we who live and die in a meaningless instant of eternity—why would God regard us with such adoration? For thirty-five years there was a place deep within my soul that was troubled by that question.

Then I held Sarah Carolyn in my arms.

The tiny pair of eyes into which I gazed were unknowing, unjoyful, unrecognizing. At that moment she was capable of offering me no gift other than her mere existence. She was pink and puffy; she was wrinkly and wet; she was bellowing and bloody and not particularly impressed to meet the co-author of her conception.

None of that mattered. This child was the center of my universe. Here in my arms was a living creature Gayle and I had brought into the world, a miniature incarnation of the powerful union and love we shared in our marriage. Here was Gayle and I become one flesh, a mystery for a lifetime of delight.

What did it matter whether this child could give me anything other than a wet diaper? That was a moot point in the matter of my love for her, which would be absolute, forever and unconditional.

Then somehow, as these feelings of unquenchable love washed over me and baptized me into parenthood, somehow I heard the echo of the old question: "Why would God love anyone like me?"

Excuse me? That thought was delivered to the wrong address, surely. It had nothing to do with here and now. Yet for a fleeting instant, did I hear a voice, small yet audible in the din of a busy operating room? And if so, did the voice contain a hint of laughter?

And did I also faintly hear something else? Did I hear, "Now can you understand?"

And I had to whisper back that yes, for the first time in my life, I could. I really could.

THE GREAT
ELF DISASTER

Christmas may well be the ultimate time for family. But sometimes our families are more far-flung than we realize. I found that out during the holiday season of 1999.

The season begins earlier and earlier when you have children. It was about August when my son brought me his Santa list. Robert was six, a bright first-grader, and he was perfectly in tune with the merchandising mandates of his generation. This was the big year of the Color Gameboy.

Robert breathlessly pointed out the toy on TV commercials and clued me in that here, in this tiny specimen of imported electronic bliss, lay the essential hope of personal contentment to cherish in his bosom for the holiday season. Wasn't it logical to assume that a loving Santa would, on Christmas morning, glad-heartedly provide this most coveted of all possible prizes—along with any accompanying software and peripherals? In that eventuality Robert, filled with euphoric wonder, would ask nothing more of life. Or words to that effect. He may not have said it in exactly that way.

Like any modern parent, I immediately wondered how much therapy would be required for my son if I denied him this toy—and how much therapy would be required for me if I had to keep hearing about Color Gameboys.

I remember the stories of the lengths my parents went to in order to avoid seeing my fragile little psyche left in ruins at the foot of the Christmas tree. When I was too young to talk, my older brother often served as an interpreter. I would murmur some gibberish, and Jim would say, "He says he has to go to the potty." Or whatever. On this occasion, Jim was interpreting for the department store Santa. "He says he wants the pirate ship," Jim stated. He went into great detail describing a wonderful little sea vessel filled with colorful pirates. One pirate even took a bath, Jim translated.

Mom and Dad must have gone to every toy store in Atlanta, asking, "Do you have that pirate ship? The one where the little pirate takes a bath?" After hours of fruitless searching, they asked Jim if there was anything else he could tell them about the pirate ship. "Oh, there isn't one, really," he said. "Rob just makes stuff up." There never had been any pirate ship.

In fairness, Jim was right about me making stuff up, including various and sundry details of this chapter.

But there was indeed such a thing as a Color Gameboy—and this Christmas season, every boy and girl wanted one. Thus I set out on a quest through the savage wastelands of Retail America. I visited all the major stores. The Color Gameboy was this year's Cabbage Patch doll—it simply wasn't to be had. Parents were whipped into a mad shopping frenzy.

I, too, was grimly determined to find the elusive chunk of circuitry. No son of mine would be a pariah in his first-grade class. So I trafficked in the black market and approached furtive characters with names like Fast Louie in downtown alleys.

Weeks passed and still, no Color Gameboy. In time, during those desperate months, I became part of a close-knit mob that assembled in the parking lots of various department stores and commercial boutiques just before the crack of dawn. We'd smile palely and greet each other as a fraternity of seekers, always knowing that, should a single Gameboy flash before our eyes, we would become a howling mob ready to trample each other.

The purported reason for the shortage was that a manufacturing plant in Taiwan had blown up—true story. This was December of 1999, and the World Gameboy Crisis, in close association with Y2K, promised to finish off civilization as we knew it. Some of my parking lot buddies insisted that the Color Gameboy was mentioned in the book of Revelation.

Sensing defeat, I struggled with what to tell my trusting son. The whole situation was further intensified by the fact that, this Christmas, the Santa story was on shaky ground in our household. If you're a veteran parent, you've lived through that year. Robert and his parents had worked out a kind of "don't ask, don't tell" policy about Santa. After the tooth fairy and the Easter bunny have been debunked, the domino effect sets in. My kids were clinging by a thread to that last illusion of childhood. I told myself that next year we would come clean on the whole Santa thing; sure, that was the ticket: *next year.*

Finally I approached Robert while he was performing some routine maintenance checks on his Hot Wheels. "Robert," I began, "you need to be aware that things are looking bad on the Color Gameboy front."

His eyes were filled with fear and disbelief as he asked me to explain. "But I asked Santa," he said. "His elves will *make* a Color Gameboy for me."

"The elves just can't keep up with the demand," I stammered. "Robert, there are boys and girls all over the *world* who want Color Gameboys."

Robert considered that point for a moment. "Daddy, have all those boys and girls behaved better than me this year? You told me I was the best little boy in the world."

I gulped. "Um, yes, I did say that, didn't I?" I gulped again; it felt like a Color Gameboy was lodged in my throat. "Well, okay," I went on, pulling Robert into my lap. "I guess you deserve to know the truth. A factory blew up—in Taiwan, they say. I didn't want to tell you the whole thing this way, you know, um, the truth about Santa and all (gulp, cough)."

"Yes, Daddy? What do you mean?" Robert's eyes were

huge and innocent. He suddenly looked very much like one of those Precious Moments figurines, perhaps one entitled "His Last Innocent Illusion, Demolished."

I chose my words carefully. "Well, son, the truth is—the truth is that, well, all these toys really come from . . . um, elves in Taiwan. Yes. And their whole factory blew up. It was on CNN. Listen, Robert, I gotta go grout the bathroom tile. Guess I'll catch you later."

"But Daddy, you always said the elves worked at the North Pole. Last year you said . . ."

"I know what I said, and it's strictly true of your traditional working elf. But your Color Gameboys, your action figures, well, these are made overseas by, um, well, *sweatshop* elves. These days Santa has to outsource certain specialized work orders, you see, and . . ."

"But how did the elf factory explode, Daddy?" Robert interrupted, fighting the tears.

See what I mean? The whole thing is a theological minefield. How had I talked myself into such a corner? I had figured we could at least wait until Christmas morning before Robert's delicate psyche was scarred for life.

"Well, I don't have all the facts of the tragedy, son, but what counts is that these courageous elves gave their lives for the electronic gaming industry. You and I need to think about their little bereaved elf families whenever we're tempted to whine and snivel about, oh, some electronic gaming console, for instance."

Robert's lower lip began to tremble. Maybe I had laid it on a bit too thick. I tried to throw out a shred of hope for the little fellow. "Robert, remember that Christmas when you were three, and Santa couldn't get you the Tickle Me Elmo? I checked today, and Santa's Web page says the Elmos are in stock now at 30 percent off retail, shipping UPS ground in twenty-four hours!"

This was strangely unhelpful. Robert left the room whimpering. I got in trouble with his mommy, of course. Kids and mommies, their ways are inscrutable to me.

I was working at the computer a day or two later, shopping online for an I-Can-Read book on How to Deal with Grief Over the Loss of a Fantasy Character, when I received an amazing message.

I had shared via e-mail with my extended family and friends all that you've read up to this point. One of Gayle's coworkers had forwarded the story to a brother in Montana who had driven to a store and bought a Color Gameboy for us. Just like that. He wanted to know what games we wanted with our console, and he'd have the whole package on its way to us Next Day Air.

My extended family, it turned out, was more extended than I had ever suspected.

On Christmas morning, Robert wasn't surprised in the least to see a brand-new Color Gameboy. "I knew Santa wouldn't let me down," he said with a cutting glance in my direction. "Elves in Taiwan—*boy*, Daddy, your jokes are pretty lousy."

There wasn't much I could say. I was just glad the whole thing worked out. I had learned my lessons:

1. Your family is bigger than you think.

2. In e-mail, the e is for elf.

3. The real elves live in Montana.

II

A CHRISTMAS GIFT
FOR MRS. NYE

It was the night before Christmas, and I was running on empty. I had no more fuel for Yule. As we pulled out of the driveway, I grumbled to my wife, "Tell me again why we have to go visit this Mrs. . . . what's her name?"

"Mrs. Nye," Gayle informed me patiently, for at least the third time. "We have gifts for her. It's on the way to Mother's, and we'll be in and out quickly—it won't take more than a minute or two, if you can possibly endure the experience."

You have to understand: my little family works through three households and one church every Christmas Eve. We take the approach that you *can* please all the people all the time, and we try to make like Santa and be everywhere in one night. There's dinner here, presents there, a drop-in somewhere else and a midnight candlelight service.

Next morning, at the first rays of daylight, our children somehow drag us from bed. From there, it takes us 364 days to recover and be ready for the next holiday ordeal.

The year we visited Mrs. Nye, I was already exhausted on the afternoon of Christmas Eve. I was in no wise thrilled to be adding a new activity, especially because this was also the year when Gayle's mother had recently fallen and broken her foot. She'd been shuttled from a hospital to a rehabilitation center to her present room at a care facility. As a matter of fact, that's how we had met Mrs. Nye. She had been my mother-in-law's roommate at the rehabilitation center.

This year we needed to pick up Gayle's mother from the care facility, gobble down dinner, then work rapidly through the first wave of gifts. Then we were to rocket frantically to my aunt's house. All this, and my wife wanted to pay a surplus social call to someone named Mrs. Nye?

Weeks ago, when the elderly woman had been rooming

with Gayle's mother, my wife and kids had befriended her
and learned a bit of her story. We knew that Mrs. Nye never
seemed to have any visitors, even during the Christmas season. No bright cards were taped to the wall above her bed.
She had adult children, but some unknown dispute had estranged them from her, and now they paid her as little attention as possible.

The lonely Mrs. Nye had taken a great interest in Gayle,
and particularly in Sally and Robert, who were four and two
that year. Because Gayle's mother had been transferred to
the newer facility, Mrs. Nye had the room to herself. And
there she was this evening, spending Christmas alone in a
darkened medical facility.

Christmas Eve often has an expectant silence about it.
But I noticed this evening, as we entered the corridor, a
stillness that was a bit unsettling; so much bland institu-
tional sterility for a time of warmth and celebration and
sentiment. Surely this was no evening to spend alone. Yet
not a creature was stirring in this particular ward—not
even a nurse.

Mrs. Nye was in her gown and slippers, watching a game
show on the room's TV monitor as we arrived. Sally and
Robert burst into her room, laughing as they teased her

with a grocery bag full of gifts. The gifts were simple: basic items of clothing Gayle had noticed that Mrs. Nye needed. But my wife had wrapped them up brightly. Sally and Robert handed each package to their new friend. And I'll never forget the old woman's reception of them.

To begin with, Mrs. Nye was completely startled, her eyes wide. Then she began to laugh gently as a tear wandered down her cheek. Sally and Robert stared, mystified as to why anyone would cry while receiving gifts. Mrs. Nye reached for the two of them and crushed them to her, saying, "I can't believe you really came to see me on Christmas Eve. I just can't believe it." A royal delegation from Buckingham Palace would have surprised her no more than this, our unruly little family.

Then the elderly woman turned to her packages. As she opened them—undergarments, a simple frock—you'd have thought they were precious jewels. Could it be such a rarity for her to receive Christmas gifts?

After thanking us for what must have been the eleventh time, Mrs. Nye carefully put her treasures away and returned her full attention to the kids. She teased Sally about Santa and squeezed Robert tightly in her lap. The touch of a child seemed to be an extravagant luxury for her, even as she knew we had a busy evening and couldn't linger for long. Mrs. Nye soaked in every moment of our visit and expressed many variations on the same thought: how much it meant to have a Christmas visitor.

As we made our way to the door, I realized I was no longer in so much of a hurry; it seemed more important not to leave a lonely human creature alone in a bleak ward. It was Gayle who bundled the kids back into their coats. Then we were exchanging hugs, waving goodbye, driving away, sliding back into our careful holiday itinerary. I was telling Gayle how much I'd enjoyed the visit after all and thanking her for insisting we carry it out. "I hope Mrs. Nye never again has such a lonely Christmas," I said.

"She won't," said Gayle. "She'll never have another one at all."

"What do you mean?"

Gayle looked at me curiously. "I thought I told you," she said, "Mrs. Nye is in the final stages of her illness. This will be her last holiday season."

I sank back into my seat, devastated, letting Gayle's words sink in. The worst part was knowing Gayle had undoubtedly told me these things before. As usual I'd been too busy with my own urgent concerns for the meaning to register. I hadn't known Mrs. Nye; why should I have paid any particular notice?

But I knew her now, and it pained me to think about this. Mrs. Nye had taken in how many Christmases? Seventy-five, eighty? And we'd just now had the task—no, the breathtaking honor and privilege—of providing just a tiny gesture of love and care upon the event of her final Christmas Eve. It occurred to me that perhaps God had sent messengers on a mission of grace, and Mrs. Nye recognized it. I did not.

The rest of the evening would be a bittersweet one for me, especially surrounded by the happy chaos of family laughter that could not penetrate my sober reflection. I thought of the simple, shining lesson buried beneath the holiday uproar. Occasionally that stubborn truth somehow manages to peek through the tinsel, and its sharp light always startles me. Why do we keep forgetting?

For a dying, estranged woman, the real gift wasn't wrapped. It was the sharing of our children—innocent, affectionate children. The gift was for her to be part of a family again, if only for a few minutes and if only for one final encore. Here, once again, was the timeless reality of Christmas, playing out in infinite variations, always echoing the gift given two thousand years ago, when another child was shared with a dying, estranged world—the Child's simple, unanticipated visit to one of the planet's dark and forgotten corridors.

The presentation of a child is the shocking gift of springtime to winter's killing frost; the infant to the aged; rejuvenated life to impending death. Echoes of the Christ-gift can be heard and traces of it seen all around us if we'll only open our eyes to look and our ears to listen. In every season the truth is before us, but never, perhaps, so much as in the midst of bleak midwinter, when the contrast and the irony are all around us: an evergreen in snow, life in death.

I realized once again that my family was larger than my feeble vision allowed. Mrs. Nye is my family. Every lonely, hurting creature is my family. And when I refuse to acknowledge it, I suffer a loss as great as that of the one I am sent to comfort.

I can't recall what gifts I bought or unwrapped that year when Sally was four and Robert two. I have forgotten every single one of them. But I know for certain that was the Christmas when I received the richest gift of them all—the one I must never forget, for it holds within it the tiny, sparkling mystery of Christmas.

Thank you, Mrs. Nye, for your gift. I look forward to the

day when we'll celebrate with you again, my friend—not on a Christmas Eve in a cold corridor, but in a world where every day is Christmas morning, where every tear has been wiped away and where the gates of forever give way to the undimmed celebration of a family reunion beyond our greatest dreams.